To—

Hope & my book!.

Bob

'CAN'T TALK,

CAN THINK,

CAN WRITE!'

Published by

Cauliay Publishing & Distribution
PO Box 12076
Aberdeen
AB16 9AL
www.cauliaybooks.com

First Edition
ISBN 978-0-9568810-2-1
Copyright © Robert Morrison 2011
Cover design by © Cauliay Publishing
Cover photograph by Evelyn Morrison

A CIP catalogue record for this book is available from the British Library.

For granny Shaw (15th May 1933 - 6th November 2008), mum, dad & Kerry and my friends, I couldn't have done this or be where I am without you.

Foreword

For several years now, Bill Kelly and his family of 'Better Read' books in Ellon have hosted regular literary evenings. It has been a privilege while attending these evenings to have seen Robert change from a shy, hesitant character to the self-confident, assured performer he has become today. Poetry, in essence, is a medium for story-telling and Robert has certainly mastered that aspect. His poetry ranges from the whimsical to the profound, the contents of which will appeal to all tastes and as an avid fan, I can thoroughly recommend his work to the reader.

Alan Barker, July 2011.

Introduction

I was born in Inverness in 1982. I'm very proud of my Scottish heritage, I am also proud to call myself British. I moved through to Ellon, Aberdeenshire, when I was about nine months old and have lived here ever since. I have happy memories of childhood. I can still picture the open plan classrooms, in Primary School, and smell the floor of the gym. I remember art and baking and Maths and English, as well as the cartoons and parties at Christmas. At Academy I developed my love of Biology and History, and a loathing for cross country running! I'm proud to have left as part of the 'class of 2000' and I'm equally proud to have attained an honours degree, in Zoology, from the University of Aberdeen, graduating in 2004. I worked for ten and a half years in a local supermarket; and the main thing that I took away, from all those years working, was the people I met, both staff and customers. I have made lifelong friends, people who are dear to my heart. That's what matters most to me.

When I was aged 26, I was diagnosed with Asperger's. There were times before then that I felt like I'd fallen down a dark abyss. It was like I didn't know my own mind or what to think anymore and I didn't know what to say when I spoke. I couldn't talk and yet I wanted to, and had plenty to say. That's when I discovered poetry as a form of expression. I just wrote down what I felt, it came out of my head so easily and I've gone on from there. I write about how something makes me feel - that may be something I've heard, seen or experienced; anything that has happened in life, either in the world or to me personally. That is my inspiration. In a way my Asperger's has fuelled my writing and my writing has alleviated my Asperger's, so they are both linked intricately together in my life. Poetry has helped me to express myself and it's helped me to get better at talking to people. I don't see my Asperger's as a struggle at all, I might have done once, but not anymore. I don't even see it as a 'syndrome'. It's a challenge, but that's what life is all about, challenges. This is one of the biggest that I've been given, but I'll win it, I already am winning it, every day! I'd like to challenge some of the perceptions of Asperger's, which is why you won't see me using any words like syndrome, disorder, disease, normal, medication or cure or suchlike. These are all negatives that we need to get away from. Whatever challenge you face personally, in your life, my message is that you can get there, you can do anything!

I don't just write poetry for myself. I write it for others. I hope, therefore, that people will find something for themselves, a unique meaning of their own in my poems. If I've given someone that, be that in the form of comfort or the occasional chuckle or something else entirely, that they needed to feel, then I have succeeded when I wrote my poetry and gave it out to others to read or hear. Above all, I'd really like to give some inspiration to anyone who is struggling in their life, for whatever reason. That's why I write!

This is a very personal journey. My poetry reveals so much about me that it's a biography of sorts and that is how it should be. Typically me, and many will laugh, I've organised my poems, in great detail, into subjects that are important to me. I'd like to think you could read them from cover to cover, or just browse through them in any order you please. I hope that if you are looking for a particular poem, then you will find it in one of these and enjoy my poetry. Happy reading to every one!

Thanks

While I have developed a deep strength within myself, and a strong self-belief and self-confidence, on my own, there are a number of people that have been an amazing help along the way, and it would be wrong of me to forget them.

My family have always been there for me, supporting and encouraging me, particularly my mum, dad and sister Kerry, even when I've been grumpy and difficult to tolerate, so a massive thank you to them! Also a thank you to mum and dad for proof reading the text for me!

I am blessed with many wonderful friends who have listened and been there for me through thick and thin. They each mean the world to me, many of them have inspired poems in this book and, if I haven't always shown it, I'd like to say thank you. If you're reading this, you each know who you are!

Thank you to Alan Barker, for regularly reading anything I've written, offering his opinions and his encouragement and for providing a few words for this book.

To Bill Kelly and family, Better Read Books, and the people who attend 'the Better Read Poetry Evenings', I would like to give a massive thank you. They have allowed me to share my poetry and build my confidence as a speaker. This has not only inspired me to keep writing, and reading, but it has also built up my self-belief and self-confidence in all aspects of my life. Every word that has been said about my poetry, I respect and thank them for.

Finally, but by no means last, I would like to say thank you to Michael William Molden, for his kind words about my work, offering me inspiration and encouragement and giving me the opportunity to publish my poetry and share it as I have always hoped and intended. Thank you Michael.

I hope that I haven't left anyone out, if I have I am sorry - rest assured you have my deepest thanks!

Also, a thank you to my late granny and granda, who are around me all the time, and always in my thoughts.

Friendship

Friendship means a lot to me and I write a lot of friendship poems. I'd like someone to be able to read one, or all, of these poems and find friendship here. These poems are dedicated to all of my friends, every single one, as without them I wouldn't have been able to write any of them.

'True Friendship'

I once read something
An old proverb
I think it was
That advised you to
Fall slow into friendship
But to
Keep a strong hold
Once you've fallen
I truly believe that
For those that are friends
For life
Time and distance
Do not matter
A true friend is always there
Good times and bad
True friendship!

Friendship is extremely important to me, which is why I write a lot of poems about it. I think, long after writing this poem, that the quote I remember may well have been said by Socrates, but I have read a good number of old proverbs too, so that line still stands. True friendship is something extra special, you can't quite put it all down into words just how much some friends mean to you, but this is a little poem of what true friendship, and my true friends, mean to me (and if anyone of them are reading this, they know who they are - this one is for you!).

'The Warmth of Friendship'

Well, it's
Freezing outside
But I'm surrounded
By the warmth
Of all my friends
And that's much warmer
Than the cold outside
The warmth of
Friendship!

*No matter how cold it can get, even during the most freezing,
bitter winter, there is a warmth that always surrounds me and
that is the warmth and the affection of my friends, 'the warmth
of friendship' of the title. This was written when it genuinely
was freezing outside, and I found warmth from my friends.*

'Giving'

Giving is much more
Rewarding than receiving
So have a smile
My friends, all of you
For it costs me nothing at all
Whether your day
Is bright or blue
For whatever reason
You could use
A smile today, It is yours
From me to you!
I need no thanks, I ask for nothing
Just hold in your heart
That as long as you're happy
Then I am too!

I find it great to receive from others but I find it so much more satisfying to give. Even if it's just giving a smile, saying hello or just being nice to someone, it doesn't take a lot of your time and it costs nothing; and while thanks and affection are always most welcome, that is not my reason for giving. I don't always get it right, but I always do my best to give, and this poem reflects my feelings on giving.

'Hope from Lonely Despair'

Like I'm standing on the riverbank
A fast flowing river a gulf between us
Trying to tell a friend
When not knowing what's wrong
I don't know how to talk
How to get to them
I feel alone, I feel darkness
But my friend stays no matter what
Gives hope, stopping me falling
A bridge over the water
They reach out, make the river
Easier to cross
My fears start to evaporate
I'm not alone, I have a true friend
That never gives up on me
My stumbling turns to walking
And the chance of running
Darkness turns to light
Tears of despair are now
Tears of joy and hope
(- inspired by 'Bridge over Troubled Water' by Simon and
Garfunkel)

*For my 'Creative Writing' course, I had to listen to a piece of
music, then write down the words that it inspired in me and
craft them into a poem. 'Bridge over Troubled Water' made me
think of some really dark and difficult times, it brought a few
tears, but it also brought hope. The bridge that took me to safety
was a very true friend (in many cases, a few good friends) and
that's where the joy and the hope of this poem comes from.*

'What is a friend?'

What is a friend
I've often wondered
It's more than just someone else that I know
It's a person, who holds an
Extra special place in my heart
That's what a true friend
Means to me

Of course, some friends are close
Others are more distant
But they all have a part
To play in my life
They are all important
Each has a unique gift
To bring to me

Some friends are there to
Share lunch, so I'm not alone
Others are good for a laugh
To cheer me up
But the people that mean the
Most to me are those that listen
Those that I can talk to
When I need comforting

I feel lucky to know
So many human beings who care
About me
People who I can offer a shoulder
To in return

That is what a *true* friend is
Someone with whom you have
A mutual bond of trust
Where there's an anchor
Of affection
Between your souls

I really wanted to explore the meaning of friendship. Friends can be many things; from someone you eat lunch with to someone you'll cry on the shoulder of. No matter how big or small, how close or distant, the bond with each friend is unique, you each have something to offer each other and there is a reason why you are in each other's lives. This was the first of my attempts to explore the bond of friendship.

'I am there for you'

I am not always good at
Saying words
It is often better if I
Write them down
So that is what I have done
I just want <u>all</u> my
Friends to know
'I am there for you'

Upset or lonely?
Needing a shoulder to cry on?
Or someone to talk to?
Whatever it is, whoever you are
No matter how big,
No matter how small
'I am there for you'

If I can't be there in person,
I am sorry
If my actions do not always
Meet my words,
I am sorry
But my spirit will <u>always</u>
Be there
Think of my name and I
Will be with you
You will be in my thoughts
And my dreams
You are a friend, I care
About you
And 'I will <u>always</u> be
There for you'

This is for the people who mean a lot to me; to let them know that I'm always there for them. I've not always been very good with spoken words and I've often found it a real challenge to express what I mean or feel; the words that I use here are all true. It is my hope that a reader will take away their own, unique comfort from the words in this poem.

Family

I hold my family very dear to me. That includes pets, who are just 'little people' with hearts and souls, just like the rest of us. These poems, in essence, are about family love. Each of them are different, because I've tried to capture different facets of family in each poem, depending on what or who I am writing about. My simple message is, my family, I love you!

'Mum'

Mum,
There's a few words that
I wanted to say
I'll try and keep it short!

You have always been
There for me
Looking after me when
I've been ill
Putting up with me
Whenever I've moaned and
Snapped!
No one knows me
Better than you!

You always care
You are always
There for me
No matter what!
Thank you!

I just want you to know
That I am there for you too
If not in person, my
Spirit is with you
<u>All</u> the time
Just think of me
And I am there!

I might get snappy
When you chatter, whistle or hum
But they are so endearingly
Reassuringly <u>you</u>
That I miss them
When you're not around

Just three short words
From deep within my heart
Delivered with a hug
And a kiss
I LOVE YOU!

*This is a very personal poem for me, written in the hospital,
when my mum was seriously ill and, thankfully, recovering. It
has one simple message, the words 'I love you'. Life is short.
Almost losing my mum opened up to me that, while you're here,
you really should cherish those who mean a lot to you, and not
hold back from telling them how you feel.*

'Dad'

He's a good man,
My dad, he's the best
Still young too, at 21
Well, the greying hair,
The bald patch and the nasal hairs,
Do betray that
But we let him think it,
Because it keeps him happy!
Slouched on the couch,
Glasses perched on
The end of his nose
He spins his tall tales
What an imagination he has!
And a good natured sense of humour
But his true heart
Is what really matters
He's caring and loving and
He's always there for me
There's not many dad's
Who would do all the things
He does for me
I love him eternally, my dad.

I love my dad dearly, and I don't think that there's anything wrong in showing that. In this poem I wanted to capture his good humour and imagination, along with his warmth and kindness. I've got the best dad that I could ever wish for and I'm very proud of him. There's not many dad's who would provide such a constant taxi service (amongst other things) without question! This one is dedicated to him and at the heart of it, I just wanted to say, I love you dad!

'Granny'

Granny Shaw - what can I say?
I miss you so much, we all do
You are still alive
In all our memories and
Each of our hearts
The good times and bad,
The happy times and sad.

But I know you always enjoyed
A good chuckle!
It is those happy, funny times
That I always recall the most
I loved seeing your eyes light up
And hearing you laugh
When we had just read you a
Humerous rhyme - even if it was
A little dirty!

Who can forget shouting to be
Heard (especially on the phone!)
Voice and hearing aid competing
With earphones blaring out the telly!
We'd let you read it instead
"Now where did I put my glasses?"
You would say!

The last time I saw you
You called me back, not just
For a kiss,
You liked the feeling of my beard
Against your cheek
"I always liked a man with a
Beard - if I was fifty years
Younger …!"

You may not have had
A sweet tooth (despite the
Sweety tub next to your chair!)
But you were gentle and kind and caring
Above all you have a special place
In our hearts
We will never forget you
We all love you so much

My granny adored poetry and a good rhyme, the naughtier and funnier the better! I'd always intended to write a poem about her, and read it too her, but sadly she passed away before I could. I still decided to write the poem, but instead it became a tribute and a celebration of her life, that helped me grieve. I hid myself away and it was the easiest poem that I've ever written. My dad read it out at the funeral, and I like to think that she was listening, somewhere. It was a proud moment for me. This one is truly for my special granny, loved always.

'Granda'

Granda, I never knew how close
We were, how much you meant
To me
Until you were suddenly gone
I guess I thought you'd
Always be there
And in a way you always
Will be

You live on as part of me
Deep inside my heart, in
My memories
So many times I've felt
Your spirit beside me
When I've most needed you
To be there
That distinctive tobacco smell

You were always wise, always
All knowledgeable, bad at spelling
And opinionated and full of
Colourful language!

But most of all I remember
A talented artist
Someone who was kind and
Caring and gentle
Who always opened his arms
To embrace me in a warm
Cuddle

I am so <u>proud</u> of who
You were
You made mistakes but overcame
Them - because of that
You're someone I look up to

When I told you 'I love you'
That final time, and you
Replied: 'I love you too, my darling'
I knew I'd <u>never</u> forget you
My special Granda

I sat and wrote this when I felt sad. I was missing my granda more than ever (I still do and always will). I wanted to show how much he meant to me (and does mean to me) and how proud and inspired by him I am. I really felt that I needed his guidance around this time and writing about him was a way for me to feel close to him. In a strange way, I really do feel he is around me, at times, when I most need him. He was a gifted sign writer and artist and he definitely passed some of that artiness on to me!

'Sisters'

Can't live with them,
Can't live without them
When you're a brother
Living with a sister
It can teach you
A lot about girls
(if not everything!)
There's plenty bad,
But there's also
Plenty that's good
(if you believe me!)
They can be thoughtful,
Caring and loving (mine is)
And that, in the end,
Is what counts.

I've been blessed and I'm glad I have a sister, rather than a brother. That might sound strange, of course there have certainly been moments, but I really mean it and, on the whole, it's been a good thing, growing up with a sister. We've had arguments and falling outs, as with any siblings, but that's at the centre of growing up and maturing, and it's all a part of family life. I'd like to say this one is for her, and that it really has been more good than bad; she's a very thoughtful, caring and loving sister at heart and that's what matters most to me.

'Mother's Day'

A day to celebrate
And be thankful
For the person
Who gave me life
And gives me happiness
Someone special
My mum
A day for her
Mother's day

*I wanted to give my mum an extra special present for one
mother's day. I thought, what better way than to write a poem,
one of true meaning. Mother's day is a time to be thankful for
your mum, to show her that you love her and always will. This is
another one especially for mum.*

'Proud Family'

The family was so proud
He'd taken on this big role
Confident he could do it
So excited and happy to
Watch him and film him
Cheering, clapping and laughing
Except his sister - a
Little jealous, since she
Had only been a munchkin!

*This is about my family watching me in 'The Wizard of Oz' and
being really proud. I can clearly remember that they filmed it.
My sister was really jealous, because she had been in the same
play several years earlier than me, but she had only been cast as
a munchkin and, yet, here I was in the lead role!*

'Snoopy'

Snoopy my pet hamster peeps
Slight sound or smell - there he is!
He's certainly a rodent
But such a mischievous one!
Wants to know what's happening

Curious, timid beastie
Washing, sleeping, eating heaps
He's so full of quirky ways
Many not unlike myself!
Like owner, like pet, the same?

Funny that I share some traits
With a small dopey hamster
I'm also just little too!
Man and animal closer
Than he'd truly like to think?!

Snoopy, bless him, was a family pet, a hamster who I loved dearly. He has sadly passed on since I wrote this piece (as all pet's must do), so it now becomes a remembrance of his short, but special, life. Each hamster welcomed into our family has a unique soul all of their own, they are definitely not all the same! Snoopy's trait matched his name, in that he always snooped his nose into everything, especially when that involved looking for food! He's gone, but not forgotten, and this poem offers a toast to a tiny & timid, yet larger than life, character!

'Kosey'

I lie for hours
Looking cute
My adorable face
Draws 'them' near
'they' dispense food
Hay or parsley
That's 'their' role
I ring my bell,
Thump my feet,
Shake the bars
If they don't.
They give in,
Always
I'm in charge!

*I had to write a poem as though it was from an animals'
perspective, and I decided upon the perspective of the family
rabbit, Kosey. I often find that the humour that is the most funny
comes from reality and although this was written by me, it is
definitely true to the character of our much loved, if
mischievous, family pet!*

Inspirational People

These poems are about three people (not the only ones!) who have greatly inspired me in life. In life, you come across some special people, who will inspire you in so many different ways, and these poems try to reflect that. There are lots of people who have inspired me and given me strength, and really touched my heart. The meaning behind these poems is very much for them too, and I'd like them, and others, to take inspiration of their own from these poems.

'Connie'

There was a lady that I knew
Who lived next door
She was almost another grandmother
So good natured, full of
Such affection and warmth
I'm still in her living room
She's seated in a comfy chair
The phone on the wall,
Widescreen TV and bookcase
And South African wall hangings
Around the rest of the room
She was a gossip,
With an opinion on everything
And full of self confidence
That gave others envy
One in a million, a special person

I used to live next door to a loving and inspiring woman, I used to love sitting in her living room, having a chuckle and talking about all sorts of things (from the war to life in South Africa) and sharing a drink. She was a lady of many words, who knew how to stand up for herself and taught me so much about life. She was a close, close friend, so close that I'd class her as having been part of my family. You can choose your friends and I'm glad I chose her, she had a big impact on me. Sadly gone for a few years now, this poem was written to remember her. This one is for you, Connie, missed always, but never forgotten.

'In Honour of Vincent'

An artist stared
Upwards one night
And he saw the wonder
Of the night sky
Over the river Rhone
His brush painted a
Vibrant splash of colour -
'The Starry Night'
If only Vincent van Gogh
Had had more self-belief
And seen that same
Wonder in himself
Well - I did
He gives me inspiration
And self-belief
Through his life and work
And the courage
To know that
My demons will never
Overcome the strength
Of my heart!

I read a quote from Vincent van Gogh 'As we advance in life it becomes more and more difficult, but in fighting the difficulties the innermost strength of the heart is developed' and I remember thinking what a shame it was that, in the end, he didn't find his own strength and self-belief, within his own heart. It's tragic that he was never fully appreciated in his own time. I think he was a truly inspirational man and artist, 'The Starry Night' is, without a doubt, my favourite painting. That is what really matters most now, Vincent has given so much to me and so many others. I wrote the fragment 'if only Vincent had had more self-belief... but he gives ME inspiration and self-

belief, through his life and work, and MY demons will never overcome the STRENGTH of my heart', and developed this poem from that. I've drawn strength not only from that, but from the support of my family and friends, and the group who attend poetry evenings at 'Better Read'. This one is dedicated to Vincent van Gogh and his memory. If there's one thing he never was, in my eyes, he was never a failure in life.

'Anne Frank'

What an inspiring and
Loveable young girl.
I can't read her diary
Or hear her story
Without a tear in my eye.
Charming, intelligent, courageous
And mature beyond her years
In the face of terrible persecution
Anne Frank was the
Best of humanity
Betrayed and brought to death
By the absolute worst
She wrote her diary to express
All that was in her
To confide, for comfort and support.
An intimate and unforgettable account
Of a brave young woman
Who still found faith and kept smiling
Amidst a tale of human suffering.
Anne wanted to go on living,
After her death, and, god bless her,
She most certainly has.
May her memory live on forever
We must never forget her
Or the millions of others who died
At the hands of cruelty, inhumanity and pure evil.
Above all, let us please
remember Anne Frank's
Unfaltering spirit and heart of goodness.

Anne Frank's diary automatically brings a tear to the eye when you open it, such a beautiful and inspirational person, and yet you know that the tale ends in tragedy (along with that of millions of others). It makes me angry when people say the holocaust never happened. Well, it did, and we should never forget that, we should remember it and never let it happen again (all too sadly the same cruelty and inhumanity is still at work in the world today, big or small, each life is too high a cost). The thing that touches my heart the most about Anne, is her spirit and her ability to hold a smile, even against the most insurmountable odds. I think we should remember that remarkable quality, and take our own hope and comfort from it. Anne wanted to go on living after her death, and I hope this poem plays a part in that wish, we will never forget you Anne. In memory of Anne Frank.

Me

These poems are all about me! I hope they all have a good balance between vanity and modesty, but I don't hold back in any of them and they are each very much from the heart. I'll leave it to a reader to decide what to make of me, from these poems.

'I am Born'

Thursday night, Friday morning
Sometime around midnight that initial glint is now me
I am here!
Mistake or choice
I have arrived
Quickly and eagerly too!
First sight my dad's face?
Darkness turned to light?
First sound - my crying?
Drowning out everything else?
First thought? Who knows,
I'm hungry?
A one in 'millions' of chances,
Fragile and delicate
But I made it!
I am born

Very much me, this is about my birth! I had to write either a story, or a poem, about being born for my 'Creative Writing' course and I decided upon a poem. There are a lot of questions, because I really don't know (and can't possibly remember!) what I was really thinking or feeling as I was born into this world!

'Can't talk, can think, can write!'

I can't talk
Or to put it another way
I don't always express myself
Properly through the
Spoken word

I can think
A jumble of words
What I want to say
How to connect them
In the right order?
It's hard to relay to people
My inner thoughts and feelings
But …

I can write
I can scribble, score through, re-write
Get to what I want to say
Through a story or poem
I can only hope
The reader or listener
Understands what's so clear
Inside my own head!

This is the clearest poem that I have written about how my Asperger's affects my ability to communicate, and why I write poetry. I might not always be good when it comes to talking (although I am learning) but I can definitely think and I can most certainly write what I am feeling and what I want to say! I am really rather proud, and pleased, with this poem, it reflects me very well.

'How I see the world'

I see the world a
Slightly different way
To everyone else, due
To my Asperger's
Not the right way, not the wrong way
Just a different way
It's a matter of communication
It's like being in a
Foreign country, an 'alien' culture
It's not that I can't read signals,
I just find it hard
And it varies day to day!
Tone of voice, facial expression,
Body language, choice of words
I don't always interpret them at all
Or I misinterpret them completely!
If that happens, it's best just to tell me
(or try to anyway!)
I'm a bit like Mr. Spock.
I have a calm, logical side (a Vulcan side)
And a highly emotional side (a human side)
They're in constant conflict
To control each other
And find a good balance.
It causes anxiety, it causes strife
It's confusing for all at times
It's not that easy to explain
But, Spock got there in the end
And so shall I!
That's how I see the world!

It's not an easy thing to explain, how I see the world, so if this poem is confusing in any way, that's good, because that's how the world seems to me at times, confusing! I'm sure it can appear like that for all of us, in our own little ways, at times. I think that's why I've always related to Mr Spock in Star Trek really well, because he's a man out of place; he has two sides to himself that are in conflict (like me, in a way) and he's an alien, surrounded by humans (I'm an Aspie surrounded by non-Aspies), who he's not always sure how to communicate with or relate to, because it's so very different to his own Vulcan culture. This all relates well to the 'wrong planet' way of looking at Asperger's. The key point is that he adapts, he learns to settle into a different culture and he learns how to communicate better, over time he finds a way to fit in and feel welcome. I can very much relate to this, it's something that I feel I am going through now, and I know I'm definitely getting there. I started this poem and the words just rolled out, for me it's a very special one.

'Routine and Chaos'

First I had order
Breakfast then school
Maths and English
Break for lunch
PE or art
And, finally, home!
Children's TV and homework (groan)
Before bed
I liked the perfect routine,
Clear patterns to the day
Academy and university
Were much the same
Then - work and chaos
Different start time and
Break times, delivery times
And finish times
I've had to adapt … slowly …

This poem really reflects my Asperger's. I like to have routine in my life. I always say that it's one of the ways that I manage to make sense of things in this mad world. I had that all through school and university; then I entered the world of work and it all became chaos. I've adapted, and I still am adapting, but it's been a long learning curve, one that I couldn't have managed, without the support of my family and close friends.

'Banana Bread Beer!'

Fairtrade bananas …
Bread …
And hot water …
Mashed, mixed & boiled
Chilled, fermented & bottled
Then gets merrily drunk!
It's one of my 'five a day'
You know,
Banana Bread Beer!
Oh, alright! That joke's old hat,
But I love the stuff
Much as ever
I never change -
Same old me!

*My favourite drink is Wells Banana Bread Beer, I have been
fairly teased about this by friends and colleagues, the old joke
that I used to make was that it was 'One of my five a day' since
it contains fruit. I've often been asked 'what on earth's that,
when it's at home?!', when I've said it's my favourite beer, and
I thought it would be fun to write something humorous about my
favourite drink; it's very me this one! Cheers!*

'Suuuuuperbob!!!'

Is it a bird?
Is it a plane?
Is it superman?
Nope, it can't be ...
He's bearded,
He still wears specs ...
It must be suuuuuperbob!!!
A fallible superhero
Who, despite the grumps,
Does his best
To smile & laugh
Suuuuuperbob - yep,
that's me!

*Me and a friend came up with this nickname for me; I can't
remember exactly which one of us it was, but I love it! At the
same time, I do have some modesty and not all vanity (I hope!);
I don't see myself as an outright superhero, I'm just an ordinary
human being doing my best to be a good person, trying to stay
grounded and remember that I'm fallible, with plenty of faults. I
get it wrong sometimes, as well as getting it right. I do feel that
this poem, hopefully being as honest as possible, is very me!*

'Me the Wizard!'

I was once the Wizard of Oz
At school of course!
In the Christmas play
So many lines to learn
But I remembered them all
Some were jealous,
Others were proud
But they all clapped at
The end, so I think
They liked it!

*This poem reflects my 'brief' foray into the world of acting.
Probably my proudest 'acting' moment, being given the school
lead in the Christmas play. I enjoyed it all thoroughly,
especially all the acclaim from my classmates and family, I'm
just still amazed, to this day, that I learned all those lines,
because I'm really not sure that I could now, even though I'm
older. I'll hold my hand up and admit I made a few mistakes,
but otherwise it's three cheers all round.*

Emotions & Feelings

You should never shy away from emotions and feelings, and for that reason they are infused in all my poetry, particularly those here. Too many times I have held back my emotions and feelings. I want these poems to show that it is right to show them and that they are both an important part of being human.

'Not Fine'

I started thinking
Why when someone asks
"How are you today?"
Do I always automatically reply
'I'm fine, I'm happy'
When a lot of the time
I'm anything but

The truth is, I get down like
Everyone else
I work hard, I put my back out
I do more than my job entails
But I don't get paid for it
And I get very little thanks
I think, was it really worth
The bother?

There's a girl I really like
A close friend, someone who listens
Someone who always cheers me up
But I never quite have the courage
To tell her how I really feel
And that hurts, that upsets me

So next time someone asks
Maybe I'll reply:
"I'm better for knowing you care
But really I'm not happy,
I'm <u>not</u> fine at all"

This was written when work was really getting me down and, on top of that, there was a girl who I really liked, yet I couldn't pluck up the words to tell her or ask her out. I wondered why I always seemed to reply 'I'm fine', when people asked me how I was. A lot of the time I really wasn't 'fine' and I started to think, maybe I should just be honest and say that I'm not ok. I've learned that honesty is always the best thing. Just say how you 'feel' and in the long term, you can't go far wrong.

'Emotion'

Sometimes I think I'm weak
For showing so much emotion
But it's part of who I am
Deep down inside I think it
Actually makes me stronger
It's better to get it out
Than bottle it up
It's good to laugh and cry
And shout!
It's part of being human
And it's how our soul learns,
So it can evolve
And 'Move on'

I am an emotional person and I think it would be wrong for me not to show that. I'll cry just as easily as I'll laugh. Emotions are an important part of who we are as people and I believe that we should show them and not be afraid of doing so. Happy or sad, it is perfectly normal to show that we have feelings, and that they are affected by the people and events around us.

'Self-Belief'

At the end of the day
While others can help
Self-belief can only
Really come from within
It's about attitude
It's about positivity
In the face of adversity
There's no such thing
As the words 'I can't'
Merely 'I won't'
Have the mindset
'I can have a go'
You might win, you might lose
At least you'll have tried
Life isn't always about
Getting it right
It's about challenges
It's about failing sometimes
But, if you can find
The 'give it a go' mindset
You'll be amazed at
Your self-confidence, your self-belief.

*I've often found my self-confidence and self-belief a challenge.
I've turned a lot to other people, to family and friends and they
always do their best, and they do help a lot. Recently though,
I've realised that self belief (and confidence) has to come from
within, in the end. In a way, this poem is just as much about
self-confidence as self-belief, as the two are very much
entwined, as one, in my eyes. My writing gives me self-belief
and if my writing can be of help to anyone else, then I have
done my job, and that's an even more satisfying feeling.*

'Missing Someone Special'

When someone means
The world to you
For whatever reason
Missing them can be
The toughest experience
To live through.
Not seeing them or
Hearing them,
Is heartbreaking
But, the people who
Really matter are
Always there
They have a home
In your heart.

*I think missing someone really special is one of the hardest
things you can experience, whether that's someone who's died
or moved away, or just someone you don't see quite as often as
you'd like. It isn't easy. There are certain people that I'd
happily see or speak to every day! (I'll leave it up to them,
whether they would want to see or speak to me every day!). The
people who really matter to you, though, touch your heart and
they stay there forever. You might not be in contact again for a
few weeks, a few months, or even a few years, but the bond
between you remains. I truly believe this, and hope that this
poem is able to reflect it.*

'Finding Happiness'

It took a long time coming
But I think that I am
Finally there
I feel happy

I still have a way to go
More hurdles to jump
But I have learned to
Smile again,
To laugh - to have a
Joy for life

It took a long time coming
But I am finally finding
The state of happiness
That I have so long desired

Everyone has bad times, times of sadness and despair; but (and it's a big but) there are good times too (no matter how small) and I always believe in hope. This poem is about me finding happiness after a bad time in life. It is also a reminder to me that, when I do feel sad, I know I can always find happiness and good times again. It just takes effort.

'Confused'

I'm <u>so</u> confused
Her eyes twitched
What does it mean?
Does she love me?
Does she like me?
Or does she <u>just</u>
Hate me?
I find it so hard,
To pick up how
She feels
Subtle words, body
Language, facial
Twitches
It's all alien to me!

I translate the wrong
Way round
She likes me and
<u>I</u> think she fancies me!
She fancies me and
<u>I</u> don't even think
That she likes me!
Round and round,
My head in a spin
I'm so confused
About how a girl feels

This one explains itself to any man who has tried (and failed!) to understand how the female mind works! And for me, that includes the challenge of Asperger's on top. I don't intend this poem to be a slight to women and, indeed, I'm sure a woman could easily write a poem of confusion about wondering how the male mind works!

'Beauty'

It feels soft and warm,
Friendly and comfortable
Smells like roses
And the cool fresh air
Refreshing the lungs
Sounds like a blackbird
And the gentle chord of a flute
Indulgent like chocolate,
Tasting sugary and sweet
You can hold it in your arms
As someone who's special,
Needs to be loved
Feels contented
Feels reassured by me
But if dropped - shatters
Easily, so fragile
Beauty

*I'd almost like to leave the title off this poem, or at least leave it
until the end, and let the reader have fun guessing what I am
writing about. My intention here is to explore the 'meaning' of
beauty, as I see it, through the use of the five human senses,
sight, hearing, touch, smell and taste. This is, of course, entirely
my feelings of beauty and someone else (a reader) might
experience beauty in a different way with their own senses;
whether my words match or contrast with that, I hope that this
poem instils some kind of 'feeling' in whoever reads it, whether
from a view of agreement or disagreement. If it does, then I
have succeeded.*

'I'm Not Fine'

I started thinking once
Why when someone asks me
"How are you today?"
Do I always seem to reply
"I'm fine thanks"
When sometimes I am
Anything but?

I have bad days, I get down
So maybe next time
My reply might be:
"Thanks for asking,
I'm glad you care,
But really I'm *not* fine at all"

'I am not fine'

I started thinking once
When someone asks me
"How are you today?"
Why do I always seem to reply
"I am fine, thanks"
When sometimes I am
Anything but?
I have bad days, I get down
So maybe next time
My reply might be
"Thank you for asking,
I am glad you care,
But really I am <u>not</u>
Fine at all"

These two poems are both variations of the poem 'Not Fine'. I really wanted to shorten the original poem and make it more to the point - the main point being, that instead of always saying that you are fine, it is better, if you are not fine, just to be honest and say so. The second is my favourite version.

Life

*Life is the greatest journey of all that we go on. There are so
many experiences to have, good and bad, and so many things to
learn. These poems are about life, from my perspective, but I
hope that there is much here that others can relate to. I also
hope they might help guide someone along their journey, if they
have lost their way, by providing some encouragement, or even
just provoking a particular thought they needed to think.*

'Life is Short'

Life is short
So much time passes
Before you realise it
So use it for
The people who matter
Give them kindness
And care
Through the good
Times and bad times
Enjoy every moment
Together!

*I've lost some close family and friends, the last few years, and
it's made me think about how short life really is, that I should
make the most of it and enjoy it, with the people who mean a lot;
we should all make the most of every moment, while we can.*

'The Road of Life'

The Path of life
Is a long, winding road,
surrounded by forests and wilderness,
The horizon a distant speck,
the end uncertain.
There are plenty of pot holes to fall down,
There isn't a map or a guide,
And you can easily lose your way,
We all do at times.

If water seems an obstacle,
Build a bridge over it.
Jump over the pot hole
That seems a chasm.
Use landmarks, the sun and the stars
To find a route
In a forest or wilderness
Everything has a way
Through it, over it, around it.

I'm not struggling with
Life and losing
I'm being challenged by
Life and I'm winning
It's the greatest journey
I'll ever make,
That any of us will,
I'll find my way,
You'll find yours,
The journey along
'the road of life'.

This came from a discussion with a friend. I imagined life as a journey along a road, one of those long dusty highways, that seems to stretch to nowhere, with the horizon in the distance. There are lots of 'possible' obstacles in a road, pot holes to fall down, forests to get lost in and wilderness's that seem empty, but there are ways to get through them. That's the way life is and the meaning of this poem, you forge your own map and guide to your life, as you live it, whether it's the right one or not.

'No One's Perfect'

There aren't any of us
Here on this Earth
That are completely perfect
Not me, not you
We're all human
Sometimes we get it right,
But sometimes we get it wrong
That is life and
That is just
The way it is.

*It's a simple little one this one. I've spent so long trying to be
perfect and thinking that I have to be. I don't expect any of my
friends to be perfect, I just accept them for who they are, faults
and all. I've come to realise that I don't have to be perfect
either and that I have to give myself that same respect, and
accept myself for who I am, faults and all. We are imperfect
humans living in an imperfect world and it's as simple as that.*

'Too much hustle & bustle!'

You know, I think
It's just life
All these ups and downs
It's the same for everyone
We seem to spend
All our time worrying
About so many things
Getting up, going to work
Coming home, tidying up
And falling into bed
Oh, modern life -
What a hustle and bustle!

No time to stop?
Well, find the time!
Cherish family and friends
Drink a little too much
Talk for too long
Laugh hysterically
Enjoy every moment
For life is short
Make the most of it
- live it to the full
If I swept the streets
And lived in a hovel
I'd be happy
I have special people
Around me
- that's what really matters

This poem reflects the pace of modern life - that it's all too fast, for so many of us! We need to slow down and find the time, for what really matters most to us, in life. We need to do countless monotonous things, we need to work, we need money and we need to sleep; but our family and friends are more important than ever too. We should be grateful for them and show them that, by giving them more of our time.

'The Positives in the Bad'

Look at the positives
In a bad situation
The things that you can
Learn from, build on, improve upon
Don't dwell on the negatives
Just try to think
That when you have bad times
It makes the good times
All the more sweeter and memorable
Some of those good times
Will have been truly the best
Remember them!

I've learned to try and accept that bad things do happen in life, you just have to find the positives (if you can) and remember that there are some really good times as well. To truly appreciate the good times, you have to experience some bad times along the way.

'The Bully'

Don't feel anger or hurt
Or the need for retribution
Just, if you can,
Feel some pity
For at the end
Of the day
Someone who picks
On someone else
For small things
Or big things
Knowingly or unknowingly
Has a massive insecurity
Deep within themselves
That they feel
The need to show
Jealousy and resentment
Towards someone else
Who, while they work hard at it,
Has great confidence and self belief.
Don't let them walk all over you
Remember, you are
Better than that,
Better than they are
They are the one
In the wrong
The Bully.

This one, sadly, comes from experience. Most of us will have been bullied, at some time in our lives, at home, at school, at work or elsewhere. I take a stand, these days, not to stoop to a bully's level, because I'm much smarter than that. A bully will only win if you take the bait, play their game and give them what they want. Don't give them that. Stay calm, don't get angry or upset, just rise above it and let it go over your head; show them the better person that you are, who isn't going to react and they'll soon get bored.

'Work Stress!'

I wish I had more hours
To do the work
That needs to be done
I wish too, that I got
more pay and a little thanks!
I'm needed here, but I
Also have to be there!
I am like a yo-yo
Going back and forth
But can only be
In one place at once!
By the day's end
I'm falling asleep
While standing
I'm so exhausted
…. work stress!

*After one of those days at work, when it felt like I had to do 101
tasks at once and had had enough! I am sure that we have all
felt like that at some point and really, I wrote this poem as a
way to get out my stress and calm down, so that I could make
myself feel better.*

'The Management!'

They have one
Aim in life
To line their own
Pockets with dosh
They'll grumble
And shout at you
They'll just trample
Right over you
I've not met
A bunch yet
Who aren't power
Corrupted and incompetent
With a capital I!
They get right up my nose,
The Management!

This poem isn't directed at anyone in particular, and I apologise to anyone who is a manager! I was meaning the really high up 'big cheeses' when I wrote this. It is said that people with Asperger's can have trouble with authority figures, and I suppose this is true for me, to a certain extent. I have a short fuse when it comes to bank managers, politicians, executives and entrepreneurs and for good reason! In a way, this poem is a guide of how not to be, if you're a manager (if I'm even qualified to say that!).

'Bored! Bored! Bored!'

I'm bored, bored, bored
Standing on my feet
All day long
I'm tired too
I keep waiting for
Customers that come
In dribs and drabs
There's quiet spells
And really busy spells
But sometimes work
Can be a right drag
I'm Bored! Bored! Bored!

This poem evolved out of a quiet spell at work and having nothing much to do! There is nothing worse, in my eyes, in those long, silent moments, it makes your working day take that much longer to pass. On the plus side, I passed the time by writing this poem, so not all was lost.

'The Hand Scrubber'

He washed his hands hourly
each time before he got going
It always happened daily
a distinctly odd way of behaving.

Each time before he got going
he'd scrub until the skin was raw
A distinctly odd way of behaving
ending up with a red paw.

He'd scrub until the skin was raw
with the soap all a lather
ending up with a red paw
It actually became quite a bother.

With the soap all a lather
it always happened daily
and actually became quite a bother
That he washed his hands hourly.

*This is my first attempt at using 'the pantoum' form. When
learning about this particular form, I read that it works well for
showing obsessions and I thought of Obsessive Compulsive
Disorder (OCD). I went for something that I have seen before,
on television, of someone finding they have a need to constantly
wash their hands. I've wanted to try and show what a bother
that must become.*

'Snapshot of an Asperger's Man's Life'

Start of the Day

Jon did the same every day
He'd get up, then start washing
It was always the same way
And all before he got near working

He'd get up, then start washing
Next dressing himself for the day
And all before he got near working
Jon simply knew no other way

Next dressing himself for the day
Same suit, same tie, the same shoes
Jon simply knew no other way
You could imagine that his mother rues

Same suit, same tie, the same shoes
Maybe he ought to give them a good cleaning
You could imagine that his mother rues
But it wasn't his fault, it was just his way of doing

Maybe he ought to give them a good cleaning
It was just always the same way
But it wasn't his fault, it was just his way of doing
Jon always did the same every day.

Eating of Breakfast

Breakfast meant the same food
From Monday to Friday
So long as Jon's appetite was good
He'd have orange juice and a buttery

From Monday to Friday
He had the same, since he was fussy
He'd have orange juice and a buttery
Even if it didn't give variety

He had the same, since he was fussy
There was trouble if it was different
Even if it didn't give variety
It was a small price, keeping him content

There was trouble if it was different
Toast and cereal weren't the same for the day
It was a small price, keeping him content
Jon didn't care about the fat in a buttery

Toast and cereal weren't the same for the day
So long as Jon's appetite was good
Jon didn't care about the fat in a buttery
Breakfast meant the same food.

Leaving for Work

Jon made to go to his work
He'd close the doors, switch off every light
Finally turning the key in the lock
Only leaving when all was right

He'd close the doors, switch off every light
Not just double, but triple checking
Only leaving when all was right
Then he would set off walking

Not just double, but triple checking
Everything had to be left properly
Then he would set off walking
Always going the same way

Everything had to be left properly
From the doors, to every light
Always going the same way
He would make his short flight

From the doors, to every light
Finally turning the key in the lock
He would make his short flight
Jon made to go to his work.

Work and End of the Day

Work would be the same chores
Emails, phone calls and meetings
Jon faced the daily bores
That was the curse of working

Emails, phone calls and meetings
All the same until home
That was the curse of working
With hours for finish time to come

All the same until home
Day after day after day
With hours for finish time to come
Eventually he could get away

Day after day after day
Always the routine of dread
Eventually he could get away
From work, to kids homework, then bed

Always the routine of dread
Jon faced the daily bores
From work, to kids homework, then bed
It would be the same chores.

This series of linked poems is my experiment of using 'the pantoum' form, for a writing assessment. With it's repetitive nature of reusing lines (and words), this form works well in showing obsessions, such as Obsessive Compulsive Disorder (OCD). I realised that I could apply this to Asperger's and a love of routines, always eating the same foods and suchlike. This all comes from my personal experience. While I have embellished the character, I would say that Jon is a good reflection of myself, although I have been able to learn and adapt to change over the years. I deliberately kept to the same format, number of lines and verses throughout to emphasise what I was saying about Asperger's in my poems. I think it is important to write about things like Asperger's, for others to read and reflect upon, and I hope this series of poems achieves this.

'Tragedy in Japan - with a Prayer'

Shocked by the images
My words can barely say
The heartache that I feel
But - do not underestimate
The power of both
For they have true meaning

An earthquake measuring 9.0
A tsunami of over 30 feet waves
And still more aftershocks
We are small & fragile
At the mercy of nature
Perched on a
Spinning globe
That is the world

A river of boats & cars
Tossed aside as though
They were toys,
Houses crushed like matchwood
The abiding image in my mind
Of a young child,
Screened for radiation,
Standing lost & bewildered

Spare a place,
As I have,
In your heart and
In your thoughts
So the people in Japan
Are not alone
We are kindred and together.

I felt so sad, and so upset, for people so far away, when the earthquake and tsunami happened in Japan on 11th March 2011. It was a tragic event, one that will take years to recover from. The buildings can be rebuilt, but you can't bring back the dead, the people who were lost and the emotional scars of this will last a long time; they will heal, given time, but there will always be a scar that remains. I didn't really know how to react to this, but I really had to write down how I was feeling and so, as I often do, I wrote that in the form of a poem. The images we all saw on the news speak for themselves. This one is for the people of Japan.

'A Parent's Life'

The middle of the street
Alone, the shops all around
The weather grey and dull
Looked like it might rain
That would be a pain

Buggy in tow, baby asleep
Toddler clasping my hand
Stomped beside me
Didn't want to be there
The world slowly closing around us

End of the day, people going home
Seems like we walk alone
In the opposite direction
We have to go on
Shopping to be done

Every day and every month
Every month of every year
Carrying on, existing
The slow road
Leading to nowhere

Endless. Home. Work. School.
Shopping. Home. Sleep.
Trundling on to oblivion
A life of monotony.

This poem came from a picture that I saw in my 'Creative Writing' course book. The task was to write anything that this picture brought to mind. It was a black and white picture of a street from slightly afar, with buildings around it and, in the middle, what looked like a women pushing a buggy and child. This made me think of the monotony of a parents' life (even though I'm not actually a parent!) and I remembered all those long, tiring, shopping journeys with mum, walking down the road in all weathers and then back again, dragging lots of shopping bags along with us; sometimes after school, a lot of the time it was on a Saturday. I can still remember those times, especially when it was raining (and once being caught in a thunder storm!). The rest of the poem grew from this initial feeling.

'The Somali Man & The Somali Girl'

Somali man
Somali girl
Husband, wife
Two lovers?
'God said it be so' he said
Dream, real-life
End of life
The start of adulthood
Century gap
Drawn together
'We are all happy'
Her family said
She herself nodded
Eyes stared and glinted
Confetti fell
Down her cheeks
Great, great granddaughter?

*I read a newspaper article about a Somali man who, in old age,
was getting married to a girl barely in her teens (if I'm
remembering right). The article said that the girl was 'happy'
and that they were 'all happy', but it just seemed so false and, at
the same time, so wrong to me. I wrote this poem while trying to
get my head around what I had read.*

Memories

Memories are so important! That is one of the reasons I write them down. Memory is a strange thing, some of them are so close and vivid, while others are misty and distant; you don't remember every last detail, sometimes the memory cheats. Memories are the experiences in life that make us who we are; the laughter and joy along with the tears and the hurt. It's essential that we hold onto the good and, while not dwelling on them, not forget that the bad ones happened. These poems are about unique memories of mine.

'Toy Police Car'

We sold that little car
The police one with
The flashing blue light
It was only a toy
One of course
But I'd used it
Every day
nee naw, trundle trundle
Along the pavement
Feet peddling

Black wheels, white bonnet
And clear plastic windscreen
It fairly raced along
Now it raced along again
In the back
Of a grown-up's car
Going to another home

I merely stood silent
And watched
Then it was gone

I had this toy police car, when I was young, and I loved it! I can remember going back and forth along the street 'arresting' all of my friends. It was great fun! Then mum sold it. I can remember watching it disappear in the back of a 'real' police woman's car, for her son, and being so gutted, I was so upset. I'd outgrown it, I have all the great memories and it was better that it went to a child who could use it, but I still miss that wonderful little car!

'Photographs - memories captured in time'

A photograph is so
Much more than just ink
It's a moment, a special moment
A person who lives or lived
An event that happened
It tells a story or part of a story
And takes you through emotions
Sadness, joy, excitement and regret
They make you experience something unique
And something quite remarkable
Photographs are memories
Captured in time.

I'm sure we all have that album (or boxes) full of family photographs, that we take out and look through now and then. I've always looked at a photograph and felt it tells you so much more than what you're seeing. When I look at a picture of my granda, I see his grinning face and I remember, clear as day, walking into his living room, him smiling at me and throwing his arms open, giving me a cuddle, and me immediately feeling safe. I miss that, but every time I see a certain picture of him I get that same feeling and feel comforted by it. Photographs are important and special, each one captures a memory in time.

'The Journey Home'

Trains, buses and planes
Makes me think of
Stations, delays and waiting
Queues, desks and arguments
Cold, wet, sitting on a
Bench
I'm tired with lots of luggage
Falling asleep, alone
The darkness, slipping
I feel like the only one there
All I want is to get home
The journey is long barren roads,
Rails and fields, channels of water
They creep past
A gulf to cross
Day turns to night
I just want to be warm,
In bed at home
(- inspired by 'Homeward Bound' by Simon and Garfunkel)

Similar to my poem 'Hope from Lonely Despair', listening to
'Homeward Bound' has always made me think of travelling and
the longing to get (or be) at home that that can sometimes
entail. It made me think of the pitfalls of travel, and the time
when my parents were stuck in Amsterdam on their way home
from France, due to snow! On a brighter note, the poem, makes
the feeling all the more sweeter, when I read it and know that I
am safely nestled in my room at home. This one is for people on
a journey - know that wherever you are, home is always in your
heart, and there is comfort in that. I hope this poem brings a
little chuckle and warmth along with the despair (especially to
someone who is on a journey).

'Moving House'

Ruing at moving
Crying and sighing
Yet still trying
Don't forget the toaster,
When you go to the motor!
Fetch your coat
We're moving out!

Just a little poem trying to rhyme some words together about the experience of moving house and how that might make someone feel and react. Nothing really profound, but I hope the words provide enough food for thought in whoever reads it.

'Cycling Trip'

Cycling the old
Railway line
To the distant pub
A summer's day
The smell of pollen
Lots of insects
Long grass and flowers
Rasping from the edges
Gravel sliding
Underneath the tyres
A great bike,
A giant
With lots of gears
I loved it!

'The Railway Cycle'

We spent Sundays
In the old days
Enjoying cycling
Along the disused
Railway causeway

Long grass rasping
As we were going
Gravel sliding
Under the tyres
Our legs toiling

Hated the insects and pollen
Yet the perfume of flowers
And their hypnotic powers
Made us lovers
Of warm summers

'Pub Cycle'

On the railway causeway
Cycling on that bike
Now it's small
And gives a rattle
Less of a giant

The journey feels shorter
And a lot more shabby
Much less exciting
But it would be boring
Taking a car there

So cycling it is
Rather than a cab
To go to the pub
The best part at the end
It must wait longer

These three poems follow the same memory, of cycling along the old railway line, when I was younger and growing up, from the toiling legs and sun, the flowers and hay fever and itching eyes and the insects and the birds singing to the pub at the end of the journey. Those were happy times, they are good memories to me and I hope that that comes across.

'New Room'

New room, unpacked
Boxes, first thing to
Unpack, TV and DVD player
Hated the carpet
And the paper
Soon had my books
Unpacked and relatively
Tidy
It's different from
My old room -
Rectangular, not square
Now I can't imagine
Anywhere else as home
My bed, my curtains
And my blinds

*This is about when I moved house a few years ago and my
experience of arriving in a new, somewhat alien, room and
surroundings. I was the first in the house to have my room
unpacked, the bulk of it anyway, and relatively tidy by the time I
went to bed. I can't go to sleep in a mess and I think I needed
the comfort of familiar things around me. The first things to
unpack were my books, and I can remember going spare when
there was 'just' one that I couldn't find! I can say that I did
eventually come across where it was!*

The Lake District Poems

If there is heaven on Earth, this is it or at least one of them. It's a beautiful place, a relaxing place and a perfect place for me to find myself, on a holiday. While some might take photographs, inspired by Wordsworth and Coleridge country, and the world of Beatrix Potter, I painted pictures in words. I hope my words here provide something meaningful, while calming, much like the Lake District itself. I'm very proud of this set of poems, they're special to me.

'All you need!'

A pub and beer garden
Just down the road
That's all you need!
Add a local brewery
And I was right at home!

This was me, shortly after arriving on holiday in the Lake District. It was a lovely place, that eventually I felt sad to leave, but initially I felt very homesick. I did, however, feel really at home when I noticed that there was a pub just down the road from us and I discovered that there was a local brewery too. Perfect!

'A wee Wren'

A wee Wren
Sitting beside the gate
Waiting, watching, timid
Tweet, tweet, tweet!
Flitting quickly away
Hiding in the brambles
It had spotted us!

*We were out for a walk and this little Wren appeared, it sang for
a while, before spotting us and quickly hiding away. I quickly
scribbled this poem down about it, as mum was busy taking
photographs. She captured the moment in pictures, as I
captured it in words!*

'Dove Cottage'

The poet's cottage
Little Stone dwelling with smoking chimney
Postage stamp garden
Of bright flowers
An idyllic life, sweet home
Calm and welcoming
House of words and worth

We made a visit to 'Dove Cottage', the home of William
Wordsworth, and I felt inspired and compelled, not only to write
more poetry, but also to write about such a wonderful and
inspirational house and poet. I love his poetry, and it feels
appropriate to have written a few of my own, while I was here in
the Lake District, visiting this inspirational place.

'Graveyard Solitude'

Graveyards are strange places
That offer a strange
Peace and comfort
The people there have
Lived their lives
Whoever they were
Whatever their woes
Now they rest in peace
And give us spiritual hope
Amongst the Jackdaws
Chattering and squaking,
The burning embers wafting
And the yellow daffodils
Growing
Is a resting place
To reflect on
And be grateful for life

This was written in the graveyard that Wordsworth and his family are buried in. I took a moment to listen to the sounds and take in the smells, and think about the names of the people on the gravestones and this poem came to me. It is a reflection of both life and death, and how we should make the most of our lives while we are here.

'The Joy of Pubs'

The rowdy banter
Of people gossiping
Around the bar and tables
The clinking of pint glasses
The rustle of crisp packets
Even the odd 'drunken' singing
The vivid atmosphere
And joy of pubs

This was written in a pub, drinking a pint of 'Fosters' and is about the atmosphere in a pub, in this case a happy and welcoming one; having an enjoyable time, as a good pub should be like.

'What a dreich day!'

It's right dreich outside!
Pouring rain and a
Cold breeze
The air musty
On the nostrils
And damp on the skin
A real misery!
We're indoors
In a tea room
I'm gulping hot chocolate
With cream and marshmallows
Scoffing a huge slice
Of chocolate cake
And strawberry jam
Perfect remedy for such
A dreich day!

This really was a dreich day! We took the opportunity of the bad weather to visit the Beatrix Potter museum, a truly inspiring lady, I learned that there was much more to her than 'Peter Rabbit' and his friends. I also enjoyed a lovely hot chocolate, while we were there. It was the perfect remedy to the wetness outside.

'Travel by steam engine'

Looking out the window
At the picturesque valley
Nestled far below
Cottages and gardens and
Vegetable patches
Cows in the fields
Winding roads and trees
The railway line passes alongside
Steam train chug-chug
Chugging along
Carriages giving a gentle rattle
Travelling the way
They used to
What a blissful life!

I wrote this on a train, looking at the world that I could see from the window, and what a wonderful world it was, a picturesque scene. It all felt so calm, chugging along by steam engine and I hope a reader can picture, and feel, that calmness as they read my words. I can still smell the sooty smoke coming from the train. It was a lovely day too.

'Meadow Brown on the teasel'

Perched upon the
Purple teasel
A meadow brown butterfly
Nature's enchanting beauty
Sits still for
But a moment
Proboscis extended, feeding
Then it flies graceful
Winged flower moving
From perch to perch

*This is, in simple terms, about a butterfly (a meadow brown)
that landed on a flower. This occurred in the garden of 'Dove
Cottage' and it felt even more appropriate, as I outlined the
words of my poem, when I realised that William Wordsworth
himself had also written a poem about a butterfly, 'To a
Butterfly' perhaps being amazed and awed in the same way that
I was, when I saw my meadow brown, when he saw his butterfly.
I'd like to dedicate this one, in particular, to Wordsworth.*

'Moths to a flame'

I lie on my bed
The evening late
The bedroom lamp
Burning bright
Moths dance against
The window glass
Legs marching, wings flickering
Attracted to the yellow flame
Trying to get in
I can only marvel, once again
At nature's wonder
Simplicity and, yet,
Complexity
Seemingly together
At once

I was lying on my bed, in my room in the holiday cottage, and all I had on was a small lamp. When I looked up at the window, I saw all these moths battering against it, trying to get to the light, as though it were the sun (or the moon?) and I marvelled at it and scribbled this poem down.

'7 am'

7.00 am exact
I awake
Still tired, so
I went
Back to sleep

*This is a strange one, a short one that just came to me all of a
sudden and I had to write it down. I woke up, just all of a
sudden, but felt tired still and decided to go back to sleep for a
couple more hours. Before I did, however, these words just
came into my head, one of those happenstances.*

'The Fells - at the roof of the world'

Walking up the fell
Gentle hills rising
And falling
Houses and green fields and
Clusters of trees
Form a valley below
Sheep baaing,
White specks in the distance
Cows mooing from afar
And dogs barking
The scent of grass
And wild flowers
Is there a more peaceful
Place on Earth?
A calm plateau,
A pleasant breeze
It's like the roof
Of the world!
Blue sky and rolling
cotton clouds above
The village of Staveley
A toy town below

*We went on an eventful 'Fell' walk, that was tiring but
enjoyable, while we were in the 'Lake District'. I really felt like
I was on the roof of the world up there, looking down on Stavely
and the surrounding area. It was beautiful. The sounds and the
smells and the sights have stayed in my mind since.*

'The Pub Quiz'

The pub quiz
Can't say I know
All the answers
But who cares?
A few pints
A few packets of crisps
And a stab
In the dark
Might be right,
Might be wrong
It's all drunken fun
A good night out!

We went to the local pub quiz twice while we were staying in Stavely. It was all good fun, and I was even amazed at the knowledge that I was able to recall. There was one answer that was in the back of my mind, which I just couldn't bring forward, one of those annoying things, but I was able to reach it eventually. Quizzes are always good fun.

Nature & the Elements

Nature is enchanting. It conjures up so many images and feelings in the mind. The first two poems here reflect something that we can't control - the power of the weather! The third looks at the birds, and their song, which is almost constant, whether in the twilight singing you asleep, or the dawn waking you up (as is the case here).

'The Wind'

Most of the time
It is barely a whisper
A gentle sway in the trees
A gentle rustle of leaves
But when it wants to
Be heard:
It BELLOWS!
And power lines come
CRASHING down

Alone in the house
You feel trapped and
Defenceless
Only four walls surround
And protect you
As it batters against
The windows
With a ferocious 'beat', 'beat', 'beat'
And whistles down
The chimney,
With a piercing whine

Rat-a-tat-tat! The
Door rattles back
And forth,
Backwards and forwards
It wants so desperately
To get in

You can't see it, but
You can hear it
And your very bones can *feel* it
Such power, yet an unseen force
The Wind

*It was one of those quiet nights in the house, dark outside and I
only had a dim light on. With the curtains drawn, all I could
hear was the wind disturbing the silence, and that conjured up
all sorts of thoughts in my mind about the power of the wind.
This poem is the result of those imaginings.*

'Rain'

Spitting down or lashing down
Thick black clouds
Unleashing their fury below
Overflowing the drainpipe
And gushing along the gutter,
Flowing forcibly down
The drain
And tip-tapping down
The window ledge
Drip, drip, drip

The grass sodden
And muddy
The pavement musty
And wet
The hapless pedestrian
water drops piercing against
Their umbrella
Some of them glistening
Down their face
Cars wipers flying
Back and forth
A barrage battering
The house's windows
You can see it & hear it,
Smell it & taste it
Sometimes gentle,
Sometimes ferocious
Rain

This poem came from a similar situation to my poem about the wind. Alone, in the dark, in my room, with the curtains drawn and the rain battering against the window, all of my feelings and experiences involving the rain came to my mind, some of which sent a shiver down my spine and made me glad I was indoors!

'Avian Alarm Call'

It's one of those nights
I can not sleep
I've tossed and turned
To try and slumber deep
Or, I've stayed
Up <u>way</u> too late
A waste of time, it is
To even bother
Falling asleep
But! Finally! I do!
My head slowly soothes
Into pleasant dreams
Alas, it can <u>not</u> last!
After what seems mere minutes
I am awoken by my
'Avian Alarm Call'
Bang on cue, every bird possible
Seems to be singing
It's spring - so they're
Broody and courting
Then wait for it
It's that blasted blackbird,
Perched right outside
My window
I love the songs of nature
I really do
But *not* at 5 am!
Can't they keep their beaks
Shut, for a time
At least?
Then I might get
Some sleep ...

It happens during the spring, every time, that a blackbird perches outside my bedroom window and starts to sing its' heart out to court the females! It's the most beautiful sound in the world, but not at 4 or 5 am when it wakes me up! Then all the other birds join in ... and it keeps me awake. This was one of those mornings, and I wrote this poem there and then about what my thoughts were! (and I did eventually get some sleep!)

The Night Sky

I see something wondrous, and profound, each time I look up at the night sky. It's not a feeling that ever changes with time, for me it is always there. There is a mystery up there, such a vastness and, importantly, it reminds you of how small humans really are in the scheme of things, it helps ground you. Overall, I hope that my journey through the night sky, in words, is entrancing and exciting and encourages others to take a look upwards, while outside at night. It's an unbelievable feeling, seeing that dark canvas curved above and around you!

'Urania's Night'

Gaze upwards,
Night sky above,
Curved blackness.
Cold dark canvas
Pinpricked with white,
Stars shining bright
Imagine!
Planets spinning,
Worlds circling
A burning heart
Molten Mercury and sweltering Venus
The beautiful Earth
Next through rocks,
Impassioned Mars,
Majestic Gas Giants!
Godly Jupiter, Ringed Saturn
Pale Uranus, Blue Neptune

Tiny Pluto, barren & distant
The milky way, worlds
Around stars
Urania's Night, embraced.

*This was my first journey through the solar system, and the
mystery and the wonder that it bestows upon me. Urania is 'the
muse' in the domain of astronomy, with the symbol of the
celestial globe, and the meaning of the name is 'The Heavenly'.
I therefore find it appropriate that I used Urania as 'a guide' in
my poem and gave her name to the poem also. 'The muses' were
the daughters of Apollo (intellect) and Mnemosyne (memory).*

'A Silent Wonder'

Such a silent wonder
Up above
An inky panorama
With Sirius shining bright
And Betelgeuse
Burning red
Orion's belt stretches
Across the centre
As shooting stars
Fly across your vision
A special beauty
Captivating and filling
Your heart with awe
You realise just how
Lucky and unique we are
A small blue world
A pin prick in
An ocean of blackness
And fiery suns
Just as when the
Ancients looked up
You can't fail but
Be amazed!
In all those millions
Of twinkling lights,
There's only one
Of you!

Another about the night sky. It was a wondrous feeling, when I was gazing out of my bedroom window, one night, into the early hours. I looked up there, in awe, at the dark sky and each of those bright stars, so far away; and I just felt so small and lucky to be here. I'm sure I felt the same way that the ancients must have when they first looked up. It was (and is) an amazing feeling to experience and from that came this poem.

'Traversing the Solar System - In Three Stages'

The Young Gods

Journey through space
and planets spinning and circling
around inferno's heart
Elusive Mercury, sweltering Venus
and living Earth
Contrasting worlds, hidden
behind clouds and incandescence
hot and cold, bright and dark
rocks and ice, oceans and land
Birth and death
mystery and wonder,
waiting to be uncovered
Unravel this cold dark canvas
with Urania as your guide.

The Ruling Gods

Travel deep through
asteroids and debris
to fiery, impassioned Mars
and the majestic gas giants!
mighty Jupiter and ringed Saturn
Warmongers and kings
watching, planning and scheming
gods, rulers and soldiers
Planets and moons, a stormy fortress
yet silent and beautiful - imposing
The solar systems emperors.

The Ancient Gods

So far away
cold, distant and foreboding
ever more mysterious
the further out you go
towards the edge of the unknown
where the ancients lie
The ice giants!
Uranus and blue Neptune
forever frozen in time
the eternal gods that sleep
beyond them the dwarfs
Pluto and Eris
then comets and dust
the ancient, the alien
still much more to discover...

*This is a poem that I did for a writing assessment, that builds
upon my poem 'Urania's Night'. It's a journey through the
Solar System in three poems, in a very mystical way and
likening the planets to gods. I grouped them together as I saw
them, the young, the ruling and the ancient. They are separate
poems that I hope work in isolation, as well as they do together
and the last line, open and saying there is much still to discover,
is deliberate, as I hope that people read these poems and think
and wonder, for themselves, about the planets in our Solar
System.*

War

I don't, on the whole, agree with war. I accept though, that it is sometimes an evil that we have to face. In order to stop evil people, we sadly have to resort at times, to the only thing they really understand - war. It will never leave humanity, I don't think, that need to fight each other. It's a tragedy, as I believe we are all the same, deep down, regardless of differences like colour, religion or sex. We are all human beings. I think that if we must have war though, it must be for the right reasons and be conducted in a proper manner. My focus here is war in the past and war in the present and my feelings on those events.

'The Forgotten Heroes'

For the freedom of their country
And ours
The Polish pilots fought
With courage and guile
They seemed to have no fear!
One Pole broke his squadron
Without permission
To chase a bomber alone
Well, jolly good he did
- he got it!
If ever one small thing
Tipped 'The Battle of Britain'
In our favour
I'd like to think it was the '303'
Confronting the threat
With determination and spirit

They were sadly unrecognised,
Unrewarded, forgotten
And sold out to Soviet oppression
This Scot raises a glass
To the Poles, his kindred brothers
And says THANK YOU!
And sorry, you deserved better

This poem is for the people of Poland, and the Polish pilots of World War Two. I have read a lot about them and they were real men, real heroes (unlike the cowards who plotted and forgot them). That makes it feel all the more shameful to be British, knowing the way that we treated them after the war. I really don't think we would have won 'The Battle of Britain' without the bravery of the Poles and the famous '303'. This is a belated thanks, and an apology, to them.

'Battle of Britain Day'

It was September 15th 1940
The Luftwaffe launched
What it intended to be
A final, knockout blow
Swarms of Dorniers and Messerschmitts
Swept across the channel
Over 200 of them!
Two attacks - morning and afternoon
RAF fighter command
scrambled everything it had
By the battles' height
All of 11 Groups'
Spitfires and Hurricanes were airborne
Resolute, by that day's end
The defenders had repulsed both assaults
A decisive victory!
The lion had knocked …
But the mouse had stood firm.

There was one day in 1940 when the Luftwaffe sent everything
they could to try and crush the Royal Air Force for good.
Fighter Command stood up to them however, and it truly was
like a mouse standing firm in front of a lion. It makes me feel
proud, both as Scottish, and as British; and as part of the 70th
Anniversary of 'The Battle of Britain', I wanted to add my own
little celebration and, in a way, my thanks. This one is dedicated
to those brave 'fighter boys'.

'The Few'

'Never in the field
Of human conflict
Has so much been
Owed by so many
To so few'
Never have words
Been so true.
Young men, a few weeks training
And they were on call,
Every hour of the day.
They never faltered, they never gave up
They became exhausted,
But that never stopped them.
We owe them thanks,
A glass to them,
For the freedom that
We have today,
The chance to live
Our lives to the full.
The key word is 'never'
Never give up in
What or who you believe in,
'The Few' never did.

*I've always loved that Churchill quote, I've seen it so many
times, and the key word for 'the Few' that came to me was
'never'. They proved that you should never give up, whatever
the odds, and they did it when they were young, often with only
a few weeks training and even when they became exhausted. I
hold my head up high, when I give thanks to 'the Few', their
amazing spirit is one to celebrate and live up to.*

'The B-17 Gunners'

The flying fortress
Metal cage
Soaring high
Grey clouds, menacing below
The screaming of fighters
The rat-tat-tat-tat
Of machine guns
9 o'clock, 12 o'clock
6 o'clock
109's and 190's
Attacking from all angles
Relentless
The B-17 gunners
Swinging their guns
Side to side
Up and down
Returning fire
Tail gunner, nose gunner
Dorsal & ventral gunners
Sharp bangs, bright flashes
Burning, twisted metal
Those brave boys
Giving 'em hell!

I watched a short film, of an American 'Flying Fortress'
bomber from World War Two. It was frantic, with fighters flying
about them, machine guns firing and orders being barked out. It
must have been terrifying and they must have been very brave. I
have tried to reflect all of this, the feeling that I got from the
film, in this poem.

'Libya'

I see another conflict
Ordinary people suffering
More men, woman and children
Maimed and dying
A power mad dictator
Clinging on to power
Only for himself
At any cost of life
The one-legged, the disfigured, the bloodied
All lying in hospital beds
The nine year old,
Needing his face reconstructed,
That tells it all
We had to intervene
But I can't help thinking
Yet more war, the hunger for oil
Our leaders have 'their' own ends.
Don't forget the ordinary people,
Who just want a chance at life.
I have a fear, an anger,
that they will be forgotten
How much more human
Suffering and persecution,
How many more Iraqs and Libyas,
Must there be?

*I watch the events in Libya, in the news, and then think of all the
other countries, including Iraq, Yemen and Zimbabwe (why
haven't we intervened there?), and, amongst the sadness and
heartbreak, it makes me incredibly angry. These are just (for the
most part) ordinary men, women and children; people wanting
to live normal lives, in freedom. I think we have to intervene
sometimes (I didn't agree with Iraq) but I do sometimes doubt*

our own leaders' intentions. This poem reflects my feelings on a recent and ongoing (at the time of writing in April 2011) conflict.

Miscellaneous

I believe in a good miscellaneous section in any book! These poems provide a good variety, I hope, of both humorous and serious poems, to choose from and dip into. Whatever their mood, I hope that each of them is thought provoking and meaningful. If you are having a bleak day, this is a section for you. I hope that there are a few poems here to make you chuckle, and cheer you up!

'The Winner'

He shuffled the cards sharply
Winked to himself in his head
Looked at the girl
'Bet you a date I can pick
The Queen of Spades?'
She grinned, knew he couldn't
Possibly
'You're on!'
Smiling, he plucked out the
Card with 'x' in the corner
Flicked it over - the
Queen of Spades!
Her jaw dropped, oblivious
'Tomorrow night? Your
Place or mine?' he asked
Smiling, satisfied with his prize

- 'A thing worth having is a thing worth cheating for' (W. C. Fields)

I love quotes. This one came from learning to read a quote, and then write a poem, from what it makes you think of. In this case, it was a very funny and slightly naughty idea that came to me, probably while thinking about what a funny and naughty man W. C. Fields actually was (as well as being brilliant and inspirational!). I really hope this one gives a reader a good chuckle!

'Bus Stops!'

Bus stops -
You'd think they'd
Be simple things?
Well, wrong, they're not!
Two shelters,
Which one's mine?
I haven't a clue,
So I stand in the middle!
A jostle of people
Barge past for buses
First ones and Stagecoach ones
Such confusion!
But ... my bus arrives
I stick my arm out,
And it sweeps right passed!
How annoying, now I'm cross!
Quarter of an hour later
The next bus comes
This one stops, thank goodness
I clamber quickly aboard
Now I'm on it, I might
Make it to work!

I hate bus stops! I'm the most impatient person when it comes to waiting for anything, but when a bus went passed me, and I needed urgently to get home in time for work, it really annoyed me! I wrote this on the bus (the next bus, I might add!) as I was trying to calm myself down, and yes, I made it to work on time (just!).

'Pancakes - the Easy Way!'

You will need:
A bowl of cold water
One medium egg
A pre-prepared pancake mix
(well, you didn't think
I knew how to make
My own, did you?!)

To start
Crack the egg open
So most falls in the bowl
(the rest will fall
on the worktop
- it did for me!)
Add the mix
And beat together
Splashing your clothes
And the floor!
A smooth batter's best
(I admit I had one or two lumps …)

Heat one teaspoon of oil,
In a non stick frying pan,
Until just smoking hot
- when the kitchen
Fills with smoke,
And the smoke
Alarm goes off,
It's ready!

Next step -
Pour a little batter
Into the pan
Fry until golden brown
(or slightly black!)
The pancakes may
Stick slightly
On turning
(or fall apart!)
But you should
Manage to make
A good dozen!

Final stage -
Serve, heaped
On a plate,
Dripping with syrup
And with a glass of milk
- perfect!

This really is how I made pancakes! It was great fun, if very messy. I can't help thinking, however, that if I hadn't spent so much time concentrating on writing a poem, then maybe my pancakes would have turned out a lot better. I think it said 10 minutes preparation time and 15 minutes cooking time on the box, while it took me more than an hour!

'Passing a book from Person to Person'

A good book
Is meant to be shared
But what if you
Won't see the person
You want to give it to?
Easy!
Pass it to a friend of
A workmate of a friend
Of a workmate
Of the dad of
Your intended recipient,
Who'll pass it
On for you
Problem solved!
… just make sure that
They pass on thanks
Through their dad's
Workmate of a friend
Of a …

This one came from a friend offering to lend me a book, but being unable to give it to me directly themselves. They said that they'd give it to a friend to give to a workmate to give to my dad to pass to me. I said at the time that there was a poem in that; well, here it is! (if they're reading this, then they'll know who they are!)

'The Embellisher'

We all know,
At least one!
That person …
You tell them something
They pass it on
And before you know it
It's grown an extra arm
Then an extra leg
All of a sudden
Extra arms and legs
Are sprouting from all
Over the place.
It becomes bothersome
They get you into trouble
The tall story teller
The Embellisher.

This isn't aimed at anyone in particular (I'm the last person who'd want to upset or offend anyone), but I'm sure we've all encountered someone like this. Some of it's my own fault, I see the good in people, I'm too trusting and I say too much when I shouldn't; there are plenty of people who've taken advantage of that in the past, they've been all too willing, some of them! It's a learning experience, at the end of the day, it's a part of life and I try to be more careful these days.

'Haunted Stone'

The words crept across
As if by sorcery, fiery writing
Carving into grey masonry
An ancient language
The wind whispering a spell
The cobwebs stirring
A candle flickering
Shadows dancing
Black figures creeping
Across dank stone ...
(came from 'Ghost Words')

*This is another 'Creative Writing' course poem. I had to pick
two words and think of other words I associated with them. I
then had to craft a poem from what those words invoked in me. I
imagined a stone wall in one of those ancient castles (preferably
a haunted one!), with ghostly words being written across it by
an unseen spirit. I'll let you decide if you feel a presence when
reading this poem, it did send a sinister chill down my own
spine while I was writing it ...*

'The Fire Engine'

A dark, chilly night
I was an innocent bystander
Standing by the bank
All I wanted was cash!
The shrill alarm,
So sudden, startled me
I spun around
A fire engine
White and glistening
Bared down quickly
Blue lights flashing
Siren shrieking
And horns blaring
A behemoth
A cacophony of sound
Let us through, let us through!
Then, as quickly, silence forming
They were gone

*I'd gone to get money out from the cash machine. I'm a real
daydreamer at times; I was away in a dream and this fire
engines' siren suddenly blurted out and made me jump! I hadn't
expected that, just a ten pound note from the machine! This
captures that moment in time.*

'Broken Boiler'

The boiler is broken
What a bother!
It feels like
A stone house
An old Victorian
Cold room
I really hope that
It's fixed soon
Until then
I'm snuggling up in bed
And drinking steaming
Hot chocolates!

This is one of those things that would have been funny, if it wasn't so cold when it happened! I'm sure I'm not the only one who's been inconvenienced by the bother of a broken boiler, but why does it always happen when it's freezing?! It took a few attempts, but it did finally get fixed, and on the brighter side, it gave a good excuse to stay in bed and have plenty of hot chocolates!

'Chinese Take-Away'

I scurry to the curry house
To get chicken chow mein
On a rice and spice bed
With Chinese chips on the side
Is fast food good food?
It's fine with a drink, I think!

*I remember this as an experimental poem, practising with
rhyming words together, to see what worked and sounded good,
while being slightly humorous at the same time. The subject
came from my liking for a curry from the local take away, now
and then, along with a beer to wash it down. I like this one for
being short, with a little humour to it.*

'Humerous Nonsense - In Two Parts!'

1
In the restful rhapsody
Ordeal was by the omnipotent
Yet he was beautiful and brilliant
But the emotion was edifying
Could the people rectify the resent?
Their only hope was too tipsy to trust

2
It was a humerous hermaphrodite
An intellectual ready to inspire
Change the space from a shamble
But could you trust the tipsy?
Against the ordeal of the omnipotent
Make a restful rhapsody?
Just eat the yogurt and yawn … ?

*An interesting and enjoyable experiment, this is actually two
poems that I've called two parts and classed together as one.
For my 'Creative Writing' course I had to pick two words that I
liked, for all 26 letters of the alphabet. I then picked 6 numbers,
at random, and used the 12 words to write part one. I repeated
this, picking 7 numbers (14 words) to write part two (using
some of the same words) . The resultant poems worked a lot
better than I had imagined and, while nonsense really, I found
them to be slightly humorous. It was a fun method, but not one
I'd use regularly.*

'Chocolate Tower Block'

1

Chocolate block
Like a tower block
Separate flats,
Separate homes
Windows perhaps
Building upwards
Brick by brick
Light brown
Chocolate house
Wavy lines
It's smooth and oily
Clings to the skin
Almost sticky
Tastes smooth
And creamy
Gritty with bits
Through it
Crumbling under
The teeth with
Each bite
Sliding down
The throat
Chocolate Tower Block

2
Chocolate block
Rising upwards
Brick by brick
Flats side by side
Wavy line windows
Light brown
Chocolate house
Smooth and oily
Clings to the skin
Smooth and creamy
Gritty, bits
Through it
Crumbling under
Its own weight
Breaks easily apart
Falling downwards
The Chocolate Tower Block

This poem was born from looking at something everyday (in this case a chocolate bar) with how my senses imagined it to look like, feel like and smell like, and going from there. I immediately saw the block of chocolate as looking like a tower block. My initial poem is number 1, while 2 is the poem refined.

'Tower Block of Snow'

Snow on the pavement
Built up in a mound
Like blocks of bricks
Piled up high
As if a tower block

Looking at a mound of snow on the pavement, outside my work, while standing waiting for a lift, this is how I imagined the snow to look like. It is amazing the images and forms that the mind can conjure, just by looking at something as relatively simple and unremarkable as a pile of snow.

'Velvet Chocolate'

Chocolate - melted,
And flowing
Creamy and smooth
A velvet carpet
Running down my shirt

This poem explores the texture of melted chocolate, in words. I have always imagined it as being similar to smooth and luxurious sheets of velvet, in this case running down the front of my shirt. It's possible that I was eating a bar of chocolate, when I wrote this poem, and making a mess of my shirt.

'Three Shorts'

1

She asked me why I like her
I said because she's always there

2

Tree in
The garden, spring dew
On the birds nest

3

I am waiting alone
Wondering if I have to atone
I shouldn't have said it
But all I can do is wait, sit

These poems may only be a few lines each, but sometimes less is more. I can apply the first to a few of my friends and it would mean a lot more than just two lines. The second marks the start of spring. The third is the feeling of saying something wrong, and not knowing whether you need to make up for it or what you could say or do; like the first, this goes much further in your mind than just a few lines. I'd hope that these poems, short as they are, are still thought provoking and show that even short words can mean an awful lot or do a lot of harm.

'Merry Christmas'

Christmas - what a build up!
Such hustle and bustle
I'm sure I don't have to tell you!
Buying presents, wrapping presents
Tidying the house, decorating the house
There's always so much to prepare!

Then, the big day finally comes!
Giving & receiving,
Tears of laughter and joy!
Turkey & stuffing & pudding,
Wine and mince pies!
Who doesn't, eat & drink
A little too much?!

But spare the time
For a prayer & a thought
To celebrate the birth of Jesus
And the good that he brings
The hope for peace &
Happiness & well being

I'll toast to that!
Merry Christmas!
And good will to everyone on Earth!

This is my Christmas message, all the different things that Christmas means, it's about the joy and love of your family and friends, while having a wonderful time; and the greatest present of all, that the world could have, is peace and happiness and well being for everyone.

'Happy New Year!'

Well, that's another year gone
Though I have to say
It passed so fast, I hardly noticed!
Was it good or was it bad?
Whatever it was, it can't come back

It's time to look forward
With plenty of hope
And no despair
To the new year
Waiting just round the corner

Spend hogmanay as you will
But, seriously, drunk, cold
And wet outdoors?!
Silly fools!
Me, my family and my friends?
We're all comfortable indoors

Music blaring, people chatting,
People singing!
Shhh … Ten seconds to go,
I don't want to miss it!
Shouting - 10, 9, 8, 7, 6, 5, 4, 3, 2, 1!
The Edinburgh castle gun fires
Glasses clink together - cheers!!
Happy New Year!
Let it be a good one,
For all in this world.

This is my celebration of New Year, or Hogmanay, as us Scots call it! A new year, once all the fun and drinking is over, is a time to reflect and have a new start in life, I haven't mentioned resolutions in my poem though because, let's face it, we all make them, but how many of us actually keep them?

Other Titles From Cauliay Publishing

Kilts, Confetti & Conspiracy *By* Bill Shackleton
Child Of The Storm *By* Douglas Davidson
Buildings In A House Of Fire *By* Graham Tiler
Tatterdemalion *By* Ray Succre
From The Holocaust To the Highlands *By* Walter Kress
To Save My father's Soul *By* Michael William Molden
Love, Cry and Wonder Why *By* Bernard Briggs
A Seal Snorts Out The Moon *By* Colin Stewart Jones
The Haunted North *By* Graeme Milne
Revolutionaries *By* Jack Blade
Michael *By* Sandra Rowell
Poets Centre Stage (*Vol One*) *By* Various poets
The Fire House *By* Michael William Molden
The Upside Down Social World *By* Jennifer Morrison
The Strawberry Garden *By* Michael William Molden
Poets Centre Stage (*Vol Two*) *By* Various Poets
Havers & Blethers *By* The Red Book Writers
Amphisbaena *By* Ray Succre
The Ark *By* Andrew Powell
The trouble With Pheep Ahrrf *By* Coffeestayne
The Diaries of Belfour, Ellah, Rainals Co *By* Gerald Davison
Underway, Looking Aft *By* Amy Shouse
Silence Of The Night *By* Sandra Rowell
The Bubble *By* Andrew Powell
Minor Variations and Change *By* Graham Tiler
The Darkness of Dreams *By* Pamela Gaull
Spoils of the Eagle *By* Alan James Barker
When I followed The Elephant *By* Tony R. Rodriguez
Calvi Sinners *By* Roberta Vassallo

Titles Coming Soon

Grassmarket Blood *By* Bronwen Winter Phoenix
The Psychic Biker Meets The Ghost Hunter *By*
Paul Green and Stephen Lambert
The Crownless King *By* Phil Williams
The Passenger *By* Peter Wild
A Hatching of Ghosts *By* Bernard Briggs
Welcome To Oakland *By* Eric Miles Williamson

Lightning Source UK Ltd.
Milton Keynes UK
UKOW020638070212

186782UK00003B/5/P